Truth
is better
marketing

Published by Harendra Kapur

First edition: October, 2024

© 2024, Harendra Kapur

ISBN: 978-1-0685494-0-3
Cover design by Prianjali Kapur 🖤
Printed by Harendra Kapur

"The truth will set you free, but first it will piss you off."
- Joe Klass

In this book

Truth is better marketing

Two kinds of truth

"There are two kinds of truth, Mads. The kind that comes from darkness, gets bent and manipulated for someone's self-interest, and the kind you carry inside and know is real."
– Michael Connelly, Bosch

In the heat of the 2010s bull run, I was working with a startup that had just raised millions of VC dollars to build an exciting technology platform.

We were brought in to help position the business. And like with many of my clients at the time, I bought the hype. The founders were charismatic and the tech sounded like magic.

As we interviewed the executives and got into the weeds of what they were actually building, it suddenly became clear that the bit that sounded like magic wasn't real yet.

Something like it existed in a sandbox somewhere but it was still, really, just an idea.

This shook me. The story we were preparing for this company hinged almost entirely on this magical but as yet unreleased capability. Without it, the tech they were selling was entirely undifferentiated.

So I posed the question: should we really be making this the heart of our story if it wasn't even available yet?

One of their leaders retorted, "We need to tell the truth in advance." I was stunned by the sharpness of her response and, more than anything else, impressed by the way she reframed the issue.

She wasn't asking us to lie. Only to tell the truth before it was, you know, true.

Over the years, I've thought about what she said a lot.

Because in business, particularly in startups, the line between a lie and a promise can be blurry.

Indeed, in many ways, the role of a startup's founder is to continuously commit to unprovable claims about the future and then do the amazing thing of making that claim a reality.

Would Theranos have been a scam if Elizabeth Holmes had actually built the technology she told everyone she would?

Would Apple have come back from the dead if Steve Jobs didn't set ambitions that were greater than their abilities at the time?

My client ended up selling to one of the big incumbents in their space for hundreds of millions of dollars. Everyone got a big payout and I suppose, lived happily ever after.

But all these years later, I still wonder. What really is the difference between telling the 'truth in advance' and complete, utter bullshit? Does it even matter?

The long road to value

A couple of years ago, on a trip back to India, I belatedly realized that something had gone wrong with my phone's data plan. I was travelling to another city late at night when I got nervous about how I'd tell my friends when I reached.

So from the back of a cab, I started scouring my carrier's website to get some help. Every page I went to led me to a dead end. Every chat I tried to start with customer service was deflected. And try as I might, I couldn't find a phone number to call.

As I sat there frustratedly bouncing between useless FAQ pages and closed support lines, wondering how a company could do so much to evade a paying customer who needed some help while travelling, it suddenly dawned on me.

I'd actually helped multiple clients sell precisely this style of call avoidance strategy to companies like my carrier. I'd even written case studies bragging about how user-friendly the solution was, how modern it was to manage customer service this way. I'd called it a triumph of customer experience!

And now there I was, eating my own dog food, surprised I didn't like the taste of it.

As marketers, it's easy for us to distance ourselves from what we're selling. "Hey, I'm just the guy writing the case studies, I didn't start this cascade of bullshit." I can just blame my clients for creating these 'solutions'. And they can just blame their customers for demanding it. And they can just blame their customers for calling their contact centres too much.

What gets lost in this daisy chain of avoidance is any and all responsibility for whether the things we're selling create real value or not. Sitting in the back of that cab, I felt like a pointless cog in a worthless machine. Like I was doomed to a career spinning bullshit narratives for bullshit products.

The thing is, it doesn't have to be this way. We don't have to do this. We don't have to resign ourselves to putting lipstick on pigs. To the kind of marketing that doesn't value the truth.

I'm writing this book because I believe that following the truth is a better way to build products, a better way to sell them and a better way to make money. Because I believe the truth matters more to marketing now than it ever did before.

Because I believe you feel this way too.

How I got here

I first realized I had a knack for being a bullshit artist when I was 23 and studying graphic design.

I didn't particularly have a talent for design like my classmates did. But no matter how hungover, ill-prepared or out of my depth I was, once I opened my mouth in a presentation I could post-rationalize my bad ideas into good grades.

When I graduated that course, all I wanted was to be useful to the working world again. To contribute to something real.

But coming back into copywriting, I found that reality was rarely the priority.

My first job back was at a software company that offered marketing as a value-added service. Years later I would find out they were the centrepiece of an elaborate embezzlement scheme. At the time I was too naïve (and frankly, grateful for the salary) to know better.

For the most part, we did something called 'article marketing' where companies paid us to stuff copious amounts of SEO keywords into online articles. No one cared how legible the articles really were and, as far as I could tell, no one really read them.

But by some perversion of the law of averages some traffic would trickle back to our clients' websites and we would help them pretend this would eventually lead to sales.

My crucial role in this ultimately futile venture was to fill pages with words. Not to inform, not to persuade, not to connect. Simply to type.

When we weren't busy, I'd be told to sit at my desk and do 'strategic research'. This involved surfing the internet to see what other companies like ours were doing.

Needless to say, it didn't feel particularly useful. But around this time, content marketing had begun to take off as a trend. Reading about it in my downtime, I was compelled by the simplicity of the idea.

Instead of interrupting people while they watched and read things they were interested in, businesses could simply make things their prospects were actually interested in. Marketing could be effective by being useful.

So I decided to jump ship to one of the agencies spearheading this burgeoning trend in B2B. I was thrilled to get in.

I got to work with exciting companies selling all sorts of novel technologies to highly specific niches I never even knew existed. I dove head first into complex domains as diverse and esoteric as software-defined networking and micro-irrigation.

I was living an earnest dream, making genuinely useful, original content for interesting people. And getting paid for it! I was free and clear of my role as a bullshit artist.

Or so I thought. It turns out bullshit can really sneak up on you.

Burnt out on bullshit

I spent six years at that agency working my way up from junior writer to head of writing. I poured every ounce of heart and soul I had into it. And then three and a half years ago I burnt out and quit.

Like most burnouts in our industry, the story I told myself was that I had too much work to do and not enough time to do it in.

I was managing too many people, working on too many clients and in the heat of the pandemic, I hit breaking point. So I bailed.

I couldn't quite admit it at the time but I was addicted to weed and I spent the next three years hiding in a cloud of pungent smoke, doing just enough freelance work to feed myself and keep the joints rolling.

As I type these words, it has now been a little over eight months since I got sober.

With a clearer mind, I'm finally able to admit just how much of my time as an addict was spent lying to myself.

That I was doing ok. That I had grand plans. That I was better off without the people I was avoiding. The truth was that I was hiding. And the lies were merely a smoke screen to control the world around me. To make sure no one really helped me or saw me for the helpless addict I had become.

It's easy to say I burned out because I worked too hard. But the harsher truth is that I burned out because I no longer believed in the things I was working on.

With a sober mind I can now see that, professionally, my real regrets are all the battles I lost. More specifically, the battles I didn't even bother to wage. The choices I made to keep the ball rolling instead of putting my foot down and insisting on working a certain way.

If there's one thing I've learned after all these years in agencies it's that ultimately, the quality of the service you deliver is something you negotiate. Consciously or unconsciously.

When times are tough, you don't want to rock the boat. You just want the work to keep coming in so you can keep paying all the lovely people in your team.

So without ever explicitly deciding to lie or do a bad job, I let the bullshit subtly take over so much of what I did.

> *Instead of positioning businesses in the niches where they could sell the most, I was inventing categories so my clients could feel like pioneers.*

> *Instead of having difficult conversations with executives about how disjointed their plans and offers were, I was crafting grand narratives that were vague enough to encapsulate all their indecision.*

> *I'd produce content on the whims of fickle executives who barely understood the products they were selling and nod along when they called it thought leadership.*

> *I'd frame point solutions as platforms and complex services as SaaS just so my clients could tell their investors what they wanted to hear.*

> *I'd post-rationalize awards entries about campaigns based on any bits of available data that made it seem successful.*

> *I'd help new CMOs change entire stories just so they could justify their appointments, even when the old stories were perfectly fine as they were.*

> *When my clients paid for primary research that violated their preconceived narratives, I'd spin it to say whatever they wanted it to say.*

Without even realizing it had happened, I had become the cliché we all seek to avoid when we first get into the service business – giving my clients exactly what they asked for instead of what they really needed. I'd given up on the truth.

And the whole time this was happening I was making more money than I've ever made, flying business class to meet clients and giving talks on fancy stages.

Bullshit is just a choice

Now look, no one gets into marketing because they're pursuing truth. I certainly didn't. But having had the time to soberly reflect on what I genuinely believe after all these years, I think the truth is exactly what so many of us are missing.

I think the fact that I wasn't genuinely seeking truth was a large part of why I burned out. I think it's why so many marketers struggle to build brands that last. I think it's why so many agencies struggle to keep clients. And I think it's why so many people in and around marketing grow silently cynical about capitalism.

I'm not writing this book out of some moralistic sense of good and evil. I am no bastion of virtue. If I'm an expert in anything it's bullshit.

Nor am I particularly interested in some philosophical debate about what constitutes real truth. You're a grown up. I'll assume you have the capacity to know the truth when you see it.

I'm writing this book because I think an earnest pursuit of the truth is just better marketing. It is simply a more effective and reliable strategy than any bullshit you or I could conceive of.

That to create genuine value, the kind people will eagerly commit to paying more money for, for longer periods of time, the truth is our best bet.

In this book, I'd like to explain why I believe that, why it's a hard choice to make and why you may want to consider making it anyway.

Truth is better marketing

Part I
What are we doing here?

What is the point of marketing?

Chapter 1

Call me old-fashioned, but I think of marketing as all the activities a business undertakes to participate successfully within a market. It's all the choices you make to define your product, all the places you sell it, all the decisions you take to price things a certain way and all the things you do to promote it.

Let's set aside for a moment the fact that the marketing department doesn't necessarily perform all those functions any more.

What is the point of making all this effort?
Is it to coerce and manipulate people into adopting behaviours and making purchases they wouldn't have made without us trying so hard to persuade them?

Put another way, do you actually care who buys the stuff you're selling? Do you actually care if it really solves a problem for them if they pay you some money? If the things you were selling weren't really helping people meet needs they really had, would you do anything differently?

You could call these questions philosophical. You could even doubt they're worth asking.

But the answers to these questions matter immensely. Again, not in some moral sense. They matter to the long term health of your business.

If your customer acquisition costs are too high, you might be targeting people who don't actually need what you're selling. If your average customer lifetime value is too low, your customers might have good reason to stop paying you sooner than you'd like. If you're experiencing a high degree of customer churn, it might be because people are better off without your products.

That might hurt your feelings or make your bosses mad. But if you're earnestly pursuing the truth, these signals are an invitation to adapt what you're doing so you can meet customers where they are.

Now, if all you're really interested in is this quarter's metrics and keeping your job, then these are all just irritating little details to be glossed over at all costs.

And there are a million bullshit tactics you can adopt to bring more traffic to your websites, to trick people into buying stuff by mistake, to scare and confuse people who don't know better, to con gullible investors into funding your venture.

More insidiously, there are a million ways you can lie to yourself and the people you work with about how things are really going, what customers actually care about and why you're all working so hard.

In the years I've spent talking to founders and executives and marketers, I've witnessed smart, competent, experienced people bend over backwards to convince themselves of all sorts of lies and half-truths.

Some of them are so trivial all you can do is roll your eyes and hope the moment passes. Others are so plainly nonsensical that the person originating the bullshit has to actively bully and gaslight people into believing it.

Sometimes it's an executive who thinks they're hotter shit than they really are. Sometimes it's thinking your product is a bigger deal than it really is. Sometimes it's an active, malevolent attempt to convince customers of a falsehood.

In a lot of these cases, the most pragmatic thing to do is to let it slide. To look past the bullshit and keep doing your bit of the job as best you can, for as long as you can.

But all of these lies are diversions. Distractions from the path of creating real value for people who really need it.

So I'll ask again, what is the point?

A positive sum view of marketing

I propose that the point of marketing is not to control a market into submission. Our job is not to convince them they have problems they don't have. Nor is it to trick them into our funnels.

Our job is to control our company's output so that it accurately matches what the market would like. To make it convenient for people to solve the problems they have with solutions we've built.

The job of the marketer is to understand the problems a market has as that market sees them. To position the business in such a way that anyone trying to solve that problem can quickly realize there is an obvious and easy way to solve it, at a price they're willing to pay. To adapt and control what we sell to meet the needs of the people we're selling to.

In this context, the truth is our most useful resource. No matter how weird or surprising or hard to find it is, it's the fundamental bridge connecting those of us supplying solutions to the people who need to buy them.

Is the market we're selling to really a market or do we just hope it is? Are the people paying for our products going to be glad they did in a month, a quarter, a year? Are our products really able to do the things we're saying they are? Are our services really meeting the lofty goals we set for ourselves at the start of client engagements?

These questions can be hard to ask, let alone answer.

But I think we'd all be a lot happier and more successful as marketers if these were the hard problems we were tackling.

You can make millions dedicating yourself to bullshit instead. People do it all the time. You'll have to work hard for it but, by definition, all that bullshit is so widespread because so much of it does actually sell.

If, as I suspect, most of us are actually motivated by creating value, then the marketing department should be the foremost proponent of the truth. Our processes should be about discovering, understanding, communicating and responding to the reality of our markets.

I'll leave you to decide whether or not they really are in your business.

But to me, this is the single biggest reason most marketing departments are no longer responsible for all four Ps of product, price, place and promotion.

If all a CEO can reliably expect from the marketing department is some flavour-of-the-month framework, a stack of imagined customer profiles and an over-elaborate deck full of ways to spin a narrative, then we really are just the bullshit department.

On the other hand, if our businesses could trust us to supply them with an accurate view of how the market really sees things, we'd earn the right to shape its response to those ground truths. And if our markets could trust our businesses to supply them with an accurate view of reality, we'd earn their trust. Can they?

Is authenticity just believable bullshit?

Inspired by the millions of creators and publications that managed to build massive audiences out of their bedrooms, today, there is no shortage of marketers talking about authenticity. But you can always count on marketers to somehow say the right thing and miss the whole point.

Because what are we really talking about when we talk about authenticity? Are we talking about seeming authentic? About sounding like we have an honest disposition? Or are we talking about being true to ourselves? About actually orienting ourselves around the truth of our markets?

A few years ago I was working with a well-established company that specialized in helping software engineers monitor the performance of the infrastructure they built. In case you've never done any marketing to engineers, let me tell you it's never easy.

They know their craft and their tools far better than any marketer ever does, they're cynical by default when it comes to marketing materials and they can smell bullshit a mile away.

My client was one of the bigger brands in this space but had established themselves many years before engineers were involved in buying decisions. As things stood, they were being thoroughly outmanoeuvred by younger companies that were far better at talking to engineers than they were. Well, one company in particular.

They're called Honeycomb.io and the reason they seemed to be able to run circles around incumbents like my then-client was down to their straight-talking CEO Charity Majors.

(If you're interested in this kind of stuff I'd highly recommend reading Majors' blogs and twitter (@mipsytipsy). If you're not, well, I can hardly blame you!)

The issue was that while older software companies wrote blogs about how great their products were and offered detailed lists of their magnificent features, Majors was talking about the stuff that actually mattered to engineers.

She's able to do that because she's an engineer herself. She understands the dynamics of that world like someone who's been in the trenches because she's in the trenches.

That's authenticity. And there's no shortcut to it.

My clients, on the other hand, were a group of marketers who had hired some writers at an agency to write some stuff that – best case – would maybe sound like hers.

We never stood a chance.

Is persuasion enough?

Chapter 2

Implicit in my claim that the truth is better marketing is a notion that may chafe against conventional notions of what marketing is.

The way I was taught to do this, and the way many still teach it, the primary job of marketing communication is to persuade. To some extent, I don't disagree. For instance, I certainly wouldn't advise anyone to go to market with messages that are unpersuasive.

And of course, there are phases in a company and market's life where the key challenge is to persuade a large number of people to do something that they previously haven't.

However, I do believe an overly narrow focus on persuasion misses a larger point about how markets have fundamentally changed now that the dominant media in most markets – the internet – is an interactive one.

When marketers had to rely primarily on broadcast media to get their messages out, all communication was distinctly one-way by its very nature.

In an important way, the internet has turned this dynamic on its head. We're no longer just broadcasting a point of view to a captive audience. We're co-existing with highly active participants in a noisy commons.

You can't win this game just by shouting louder than everyone else. You earn the right to be heard by being something people are happy to be around.

The primary goal in such a dynamic isn't to convince, it's to gather.

Lighthouse theory

My favourite description of these new rules of engagement comes from well-known social media marketer Matthew Kobach. In addition to helping businesses gather audiences online, Kobach is also one of the more successful marketers to gather his own. He describes his approach to building his audience as follows:

> *"I try to be a lighthouse for like-minded people."*
> *- Matthew Kobach, Social media advisor*

What Kobach's succinct explanation so perfectly captures is the distinctly lighter touch required to build a brand online.

When you're relying solely on broadcast media, your messages are aimed at everyone watching that TV channel, driving past that billboard or reading that newspaper. It's okay and arguably preferable to take a heavy-handed approach in these circumstances. You're quite literally shouting from the rooftops.

Online, you're just one of a trillion different voices in a crowded town square. A few of your messages might get picked up by the algorithms and thrust in front of everyone. But if you want people to stay engaged with you, they have to get something out of it. You have to add some value to their experience of the commons.

Your goal isn't to persuade everyone that you're right. It's to find the others.

What makes your communication potent is if it's clear who it's for. If it sends signals to the people most naturally aligned with what you're doing anyway. It's even useful to send signals that alienate the people you aren't aligned with.

The hard part is figuring out who and what and why you are. And then staying true to it. People like Kobach haven't built massive online audiences with a series of invisible tricks of persuasion.

They've done it by successfully appealing to everyone else on the same wavelength as them. They published so they can figure out what that wavelength is. And the bigger their following gets, the brighter their lighthouse shines. The more people follow them, the more others become curious about how they think. No persuasion necessary.

Take this book as an example. My goal isn't to convince you to be more truthful in your marketing. I'm sure you're trying your best. No, my goal is to attract the marketers who have a sneaking suspicion that all the bullshit isn't actually paying off. I'm writing this to find the people who already believe we'd be better off with a more truthful approach to this thing we do.

My best case scenario is that by saying the things I wish were said, I might stumble into the things you wish you'd said.

The truth is a better lighthouse

If all we care about as marketers is persuasion, it's inevitable that we would rely on bullshit in our communications. After all, why should it matter whether our arguments are based in truth or not, so long as they're convincing?

The problem is, so many of the tactics that make us so effective at persuasion make for an awful lighthouse. Hyperbolic, overly certain bravado and bullshit might work in an ad. But when you're trying to build a community, they're no match for the truth.

Because even if you did somehow manage to attract a load of people to follow you under false premises, you have to keep the schtick up. It's why so many people building online brands fall for the trap of 'audience capture' where they slowly turn into caricatures of themselves for the appeasement of their followers.

The truth may limit who we attract and how we attract them. It may even constrain our ability to persuade those who are on the fence.

But in the long run, if we consistently share what we really believe, what genuinely interests us and who we're really right for, those truths attract people like us. People similarly motivated to discover their own truths.

It means we can build brands that actually stand the test of time. Because we can build communities based on something real.

Part II
Why bullshit wins

The truth is a pain in the ass

Chapter 3

So if the truth is better marketing, why is there such an immense amount of bullshit at work in our little corner of the world?

It's certainly not my view that every single person in the fields of marketing and advertising is a lying heathen or huckster. (Though I can see why some might feel that way.)

The way I see it, more often than not, bullshit is quite simply the path of least resistance.

It's easy to come up with. If enough people repeat the same bullshit, it has an uncanny ability to become widely accepted as fact. And crucially, it gives us marketers some sense of control over how things will pan out.

Need everyone aligned around a common way of working? Make up a framework and stick a TM on the end of it. Need an egotistical executive to play ball? Draw up a graph that makes your competitors look like assholes and place it at the start of your deck. Worried you're missing out on the sexiest new trends? Chuck some more buzzwords into the messaging.

Bullshit is malleable, user-friendly and available in a wide range of delicious flavours.

The truth, on the other hand, is a god damn pain in the ass.

It's messy.
It's infinitely complicated, hard to gauge and self-contradicting in a way that doesn't always fit a neat company narrative.

It isn't always obvious.
It takes digging and doubting and fumbling to find it and doesn't much care if you're trying to go live by the end of Q2.

It doesn't care about what you want it to be.
It just is what it is whether that fits your preconceived notions of how your market is supposed to operate or not.

It isn't even easy to verify.
It hides in plain sight and isn't always measurable or tangible or available in a slick analytics dashboard.

It keeps on changing.
Just because something was true yesterday doesn't mean it'll be true today. Just ask Henry Ford how people felt about horses or Steve Ballmer how he felt about the iPhone.

And it's inconvenient to defend.
If a room full of executives have accepted the same line of bullshit, it can be extremely uncomfortable to be the one person standing up for the truth. For whistleblowers it can be downright fatal.

The truth has no obligations to you or to me. It goes where it goes. Our only choice, should we choose to accept it, is to go where it takes us.

Years ago I was working with a business that had built a platform for railway companies. It was one of the early cases where someone had found a way to replace a huge swath of technical, mind-numbing effort with some pretty easy to use software that lived in the cloud.

It was several times cheaper to use than the complex, monolithic monstrosities most railway companies were already paying for.

It was an order of magnitude more performant than the ancient, creaking mainframes and manual processes these companies relied on.

And it was a modern enough interface that travellers were actually thrilled to book their journeys through it.

You would think that selling such a platform would be a piece of cake. But when the sales team went in to meet one of the people running national rail for an important European country, they were stumped by his response.

> *"So what you're saying is that if I implement this platform, I'll have more customers?"*
> *"Well, yes!"*
> *"But I don't want more customers..."*
> *"I'm sorry what?"*
> *"We can't handle more customers. It's too much of a head ache dealing with the customers we already have today..."*
> *"But..."*
> *"I'm sorry guys this isn't right for us. Thanks for your time."*

It was a perfectly reasonable assumption to build a marketing strategy around the idea that our audience wanted more customers. The truth, it turns out, was just a little more complicated than we'd hoped it would be.

The truth takes what it takes

The company selling that platform could have chosen to ignore this one sales meeting and written it off as some weird encounter. A funny story. Instead they chose to believe what they'd heard and reorient their messaging and sales strategies around the actual needs of their buyers, even though they were at odds with their initial assumptions about the market.

It isn't always easy to get your customers on the phone, it isn't always cheap to organize primary research, it isn't always expedient to patiently observe your customers' patterns and it isn't always convenient to be surprised by the way buyers behave.

To prioritize the truth is to be open to the idea that you don't know what you don't know. That your market sees things differently than you do. That you may have spent an awful lot of time and effort building a solution or marketing apparatus that is quite simply pointed in the wrong direction.

Yet as annoying and hard to uncover as it can be, the truth is ultimately what will determine whether or not your business gets to operate fruitfully in the long run.

It is tempting to control the outcomes of our actions as marketers by forcing through the agendas and plans we cooked up in our meeting rooms. But over a long enough time horizon, the truth always wins out.

At the end of the day, you only get to sell Coca Cola for 130 years if people actually like drinking it.

> *"If you address a market that really wants your product — if the dogs are eating the dog food — then you can screw up almost everything in the company and you will succeed. Conversely, if you're really good at execution but the dogs don't want to eat the dog food, you have no chance of winning."*
> *– Andy Rachleff*

The 4 Ps of bullshit

Chapter 4

When I look back on the many forks in the road between truth and bullshit that I've encountered in my career, I notice a common theme.

Almost every time I chose the path of bullshit instead of pursuing the truth I was doing it for one of three reasons. I call them the 4 Ps of bullshit.

Politeness, people-pleasing and politicking.

Politeness

Years ago I got to briefly work with one of the most well-known, legendary hardware manufacturers of all time. They had dominated their markets for so many decades that in some of them, the brand was even synonymous with the act it enabled. This company was so famous even my parents knew their name. That almost never happens in B2B.

But the more we worked with them, the clearer it became that almost everyone working there was acutely deluded about how things were really going. As famous as this brand was, it was now lagging behind in almost every market it sold in thanks to a decade of bad choices.

Yet when you spoke to the people who worked there, you got the impression they were all working at the single most important organization on the planet.

My favourite example of this delusion was when we were briefed on the launch of a new product. It was treated like a top-secret mission. We had to sign NDAs. The product had a code name to

prevent leaks. All information was on a need-to-know basis. We were a manila folder away from feeling like James Bond.
The product in question? A printer. And not even a particularly competitive one.

In environments like this, it's almost impossible to penetrate the force field of bullshit surrounding the marketing department. You can't laugh at these folks when they tell you the specifications of the printer are 'for your eyes only'. You can't shake them out of the massive ego-trip it gives them to operate with such self-importance. I'm not sure they'd want you to.

So you default to politeness. And the wall of bullshit isolating the marketing team from the harsh realities of the outside world grows a little bit thicker.

People-pleasing

Marketing agencies are magnets for people-pleasers. When you think about the kinds of young people you need to recruit to the kind of service we deliver, it's only natural.

For starters, you have to cater to the whims of clients who, by definition, don't really know what they want. But you also have to collaborate with a broad, variable mix of ambitious, take-over-the-world types in account teams and frustrated, I-could-be-an-artist-if-I-wanted-to types in creative teams.

To work in this world is to be surrounded by bullshit and ego and dogma. To thrive in it you need to be able to give each of these people precisely enough of what they want to make sure they'll all come together and do something useful.

I have no doubt that the little success I've achieved in my career in marketing agencies is precisely because of my tendency to obsess about what other people want.

But the thing about people-pleasing that I only really learned in my mid-thirties is that it's really all about control. I used to joke that my agency friends were all people pleasers and control freaks. I've now come to realize both of those are the same thing.

As much as my unhealthy obsession with other people's minds helped me establish relationships and intuit how best to serve, it also drove me to come up with whatever bullshit they'd most like to hear.

As much as I tried to keep myself honest and operate with integrity, I was also more likely than most to contort my opinions into whatever best suited the people I was intimidated by or trying to impress.

The slippery slope to bullshit is paved with a misguided sense of selflessness.

Politicking

By far and away the worst client experiences I've ever had have correlated with working with the biggest companies. That's because the special brand of Chinese whispers characteristic of large bureaucracies involves an unholy amount of guessing what the next guy up the ladder thinks.

When this fetid human centipede becomes long enough, it naturally detaches from the signals of the outside world and begins to produce only that which is politically significant.

Soon you're working on things only because Bob heard that Suzie told Roger in that meeting that what she really wants is X, Y and Z. It doesn't matter whether that's what your market actually cares about or if it makes any sense whatsoever to use your resources that way.

It doesn't even matter if Suzie really said any of that to Roger. All that matters is that the work is done promptly and to the exact specifications that Bob is guessing matter to Suzie.

Now I'll admit that this type of politicking is, in its own way, kind of fun. It's a bit like being in a gossipy TV show.

Except you're not in a TV show, no one's watching and everyone involved is so utterly divorced from the creation of real value that the company is bound to die a slow death while the executives pat themselves on the back for a job well done.

From the outside, someone writing an HBR case study might call it something cool like an innovator's dilemma. From the inside it's just bullshit politics.

When the executives in a company are more interested in stroking each other's egos than they are in uncovering the truths most relevant to their business' fate, bullshit abounds.

The truth doesn't care who notices it

All of these Ps are an attempt to control the will and minds of the people we work with and for. This is what the truth is usually competing with. The root from which bullshit blossoms.

But the reason I bring them up is because I want to be clear that there are powerful forces and sometimes even noble intentions that prevent us from earnestly pursuing the truth.

It's easy for me to write all this stuff and frame the difference between truth and bullshit as some kind of binary. In real life, it never feels that black or white. It feels like oceans and oceans of impermeable grey.

You don't get a prize and a hug for telling the truth or calling out bullshit. You more likely get glares and uncomfortable silences.

It is, still, our most reliable path to effective and useful marketing. And no matter how long you've been steeped in the specific bullshit of the company you work at, I still believe you can smell it. Even if you don't particularly want to admit that you do.

Data doesn't drive, people do

> *"Data must be used to tell the truth, not to call to action, no matter how noble the intentions."*
> – Hans Rosling, Factfulness

Over the years I've observed marketers respond to data in two diametrically opposed ways that are equally likely to result in the urgent production of bullshit.

The first way is to champion the data as if it's the living embodiment of truth and objectivity. This is the rallying cry of the movement towards 'data-driven', performance-based marketing.

> *The data will show us the way.*
> *The data says people are searching for this so we should do that.*
> *The data says more people liked A so we're going to abandon B.*
> *The data says so many people clicked on this button that it must be a good button.*

Here the data is treated like a suitable proxy for the truth, the whole truth and nothing but the truth.

The second way I've observed marketers respond to data is more rarely discussed. This is what happens when the data disconfirms the marketing team's hypotheses.

At various points in my career as a B2B content marketer, I've helped marketers work with research agencies to turn primary research into reports that might interest their prospects.

The way the process is supposed to go is that the marketers brief the research agency on the people they want to survey, work out what they want to ask them and then someone like me summarizes what we've learned so the executives we're selling to can make 'data-driven' decisions to buy whatever we're selling.

But every so often, the research doesn't say what the marketers wanted it to say. Indeed, sometimes it says the exact opposite.

When this happens, the tone of the conversation changes entirely.

> *The data must be wrong.*
> *The data doesn't match what we know to be true.*
> *The data's no good, we should fire the research agency, will they give us our money back?*

All of a sudden, the data can't be trusted.

Data isn't always truth.

Why would the same marketers who so love to brag about using data, react with such anger and defensiveness when the data disagrees with them? Isn't it obvious?

It's because they're people.

The problem is, we so enjoy harping on about being data-driven that we conveniently forget that it's actually the other way around. The marketers are the ones doing the driving.

To commit to the truth is to be sceptical when we're succumbing to dogma and humble when we're surprised by new evidence. The problem is, so often we're dogmatic about the data we like and only really sceptical about the data we don't.

Data is simply a tool to help us quantify the parts of the truth that we can measure. To confuse it for the truth is to ignore all the things we can't or don't or won't measure. And to blindly follow its lead is to relinquish the responsibility we all have as capable humans to actively understand what's really going on.

42

If search data is telling you that hundreds of people are googling 'What is <your domain>?' that doesn't necessarily mean you should build a page to bring those people to your site. In fact, given those hundreds of people don't even know what the hell your domain is, they may well be the last people you want to be bringing to your site.

If A/B testing is telling you that tons of people prefer one option over another, it is by no means a worthy substitute for the taste and intuition of the people designing those options.

And just because you have data that people are behaving a certain way doesn't mean they aren't annoyed, confused or disappointed while they do it.

Data is the finger that points at the truth. It's not the truth itself.

Equally, as people we are not rational by default, even if we'd like everyone else to think we are. The messy truth is that, like everyone else on the planet, we're precisely as rational as we feel like being at any given moment in time.

So as soon as we come across data that makes us question our preconceived notions, we suddenly become sceptical about how it was collected, what it really means and whether or not we should really believe it.

To be perfectly clear, my goal here isn't to denigrate performance marketing and data-driven enquiry. Far from it.

Some percentage of performance marketing is absolutely about the earnest pursuit of the truth. But some percentage of it is also the elaborate covering of asses. And some percentage is the purposeful obfuscation of reality.

What I'm saying is that if we want to be more effective as marketers, we need to be able to tell the difference.

43

It may not feel as comfortable as falsely acquired certainty, but I believe we'd all make more money and feel a lot better about the work we do if we accepted an inconvenient pursuit of the truth.

Take it from someone who's made a lot of money spinning data to say whatever his clients wanted him to say, it's a better use of your time.

Part III
Why the truth matters

Truth is better marketing

Good strategy starts with truth

Chapter 6

One of my perennial bug bears when I was managing a team of writers was that so many of my best people wanted to be called strategists.

They had just cause for wanting the label, of course. At least in B2B, there's an immense overlap between the domain knowledge needed for effective copywriting and effective strategy work. And we definitely charged more for the strategy work so it was fair to assume someone called a strategist would be paid a lot more.

Even beyond my team, I would often hear ambitious young people wondering aloud about how they could be more 'strategic'.

Rightly and wrongly, we've conflated the terms 'strategic' and 'important'. It's certainly fair to think that 'strategic' things should be considered more important than 'tactical' things. But it's also undeniably true that most of the things that get called strategy are just bullshit in fancy clothes.

I don't mean to sound like every strategy guru who claims that only they know the True Meaning of Strategy. It's just that, to my mind, the whole point of strategy is to make clear decisions about what a company will and won't do with its limited time and resources.

But all too often the job of defining a strategy ends up being an overwrought, overly democratic nightmare of a process that's the antithesis of actual decision-making.

Instead of narrowing our range of options to give the company a single-minded focus it can double down on, we politely equivocate until all that's left is a convoluted path meandering in a million different directions.

Everyone wants to be strategic but no one wants to make hard choices.

Good strategy limits your options. Bad strategy feels great.

One of my biggest regrets doing a strategy gig was several years ago when a young startup built outside Silicon Valley had raised more money than it necessarily knew what to do with.

I was part of a team helping to position a new entrant in the complicated world of TV infrastructure. To make things trickier, this young company had built what's sometimes known as a double-sided platform. That is, the technology needed to be sold to both buyers and sellers on either side of a market.

These things are always hard to get going because they present you with a chicken and egg problem. You need enough buyers on the platform to motivate the sellers to play ball and if you don't have any sellers on the platform, well, there isn't much for the buyers to do.

Now, if this was a well-known brand to both buyers and sellers, it would have been a little bit easier to get the ball rolling. But this company was pretty much a complete unknown. And everyone it was competing against already had years of well-established brand equity, not to mention active, pre-existing relationships.

As we dived into the research and interviewed people throughout this weird little market, I started to wonder about how we might get our foot in the door. The technology was exciting and actually worked which was a relief. But the total addressable market was every buyer and seller of TV advertising in all of America.

So I recommended we narrow our gaze to focus exclusively on local TV markets. They were a smaller and undoubtedly less exciting chunk of the market relative to the big national players like NBC. But they needed what we were selling far more than the big players did and still represented several billions of dollars in ad spend.

And crucially, this little company had punched above its weight to land a partnership with the two companies that controlled the majority of local TV companies in the US.

The idea was to spend the next couple of years demonstrating the value of the platform in these local markets until we could earn the attention of the national networks.

It was duly shot down before it ever reached the CEO.

The problem, was that in order to effectively shepherd the millions they'd raised, the company had just hired a new CMO. He had come in to help land big, sexy logos and he wasn't going to wait a couple of years for that to start happening. To him targeting local markets just didn't feel ambitious enough.

My regret is that I didn't do a good enough job of convincing him to play a game he could actually win. Instead, as a young and impressionable novice, I buckled under the pressure and wrote some exciting-sounding slides about how we could land the national networks even though no one knew us and we hadn't proven a god damn thing.

He loved the new 'strategy', his CEO said he liked the words, we got paid and we moved on. About six months later, the whole c-suite, including the CEO, were let go and the business was wrapped up.

Marketing isn't about hype, it's about clarity

Now I'm not deluded enough to think they would still be in business if they'd listened to my original proposal and the sad truth is, they were probably never going to make it even if they did.

But I can tell you I failed at my job by letting some executive's ego prevent that company from adopting a strategy it could actually deliver on.

In theory, we can all understand that it's better to be a big fish in a small pond than it is to be a small fish in a big pond. In practice, it feels better to pretend we're bigger fish than we really are.

Good strategy necessarily starts with an acceptance and tolerance of the reality of what our business is and what it can realistically do. If we don't limit the scope of everything we could potentially achieve we spread ourselves so thin we don't actually go anywhere in particular.

The truth matters because ultimately there are some people who are more likely to buy from us than others. There are some things we can do as a business and other things we simply can't or won't do. There is stuff your competitors are better at than you are. In the context of defining a strategy, these constraints are good!

It's easier to pretend your addressable market is bigger than it really is when you're trying to raise money. And it sure feels nice to pretend your competitors are a bunch of misguided dimwits.

But it's downright foolish to pretend your solution is right for every buyer on planet earth if it's going to stop you from appealing to the specific subset of people who actually do need what you're selling.

The first step to being considered the best at something is being noticeably different. But how many brands waste years insisting that their biggest differentiator is that they're best? And how often is that really true?

Is your positioning based on a categorization of the market that the market would agree with? Or did you just spin up a grand narrative to make all your executives feel like important people?

Is your brand really as distinctive as you'd like to think it is? Or are your buyers really just buying the category and you happened to be in it?

Truthful answers to these questions give us the clarity we need to effectively prioritize. That clarity helps our best prospects know we're who they should be buying from. And that prioritization helps us appropriately allocate the little time and resources we have.

The truth helps us *win*.

Truth is better marketing

The truth is more interesting

Chapter 7

For the vast majority of my career, I've been hired by marketers looking for a strategically valuable tone of voice. The idea, as people like me usually sell it, is that brands can differentiate themselves by how they say things.

In B2B in particular, we've spent a lot of time talking about how important it is to sound human and write like you talk. That it's not just copywriting, it's story telling.

All of that is true enough to make anyone saying it feel artistically validated. And I'll even admit I'm proud of the progress so many B2B brands have made relative to the impenetrable legalese the industry used to be characterized by. (Yeah, it used to be worse!)

But I'd argue that ultimately the thing that really matters is what you say.

You can talk about being provocative and exciting all you want in your brand guidelines but at the end of the day you do have to actually provoke and excite.

The truth is an opportunity to surprise.
If you're in an industry where everyone says the same things and sounds like each other, one of the most reliable ways to stand out is to bluntly address the truths everyone else is too afraid to confront.

The price for doing this need only be paid in courage. You can spend the exact same amount on agencies and media placement. But by having the stones to show your market you see things the way they do – and crucially – that your business has actually done something about it, you can dramatically increase the effectiveness of all those investments.

Avis is only No.2 in rent a cars. So why go with us?

We try harder.
(When you're not the biggest, you have to.)

We just can't afford dirty ashtrays. Or half-empty gas tanks. Or worn wipers. Or unwashed cars. Or low tires. Or anything less than seat-adjusters that adjust. Heaters that heat. Defrosters that defrost.

Obviously, the thing we try hardest for is just to be nice. To start you out right with a new car, like a lively, super-torque Ford, and a pleasant smile. To know, say, where you get a good pastrami sandwich in Duluth.

Why?

Because we can't afford to take you for granted.

Go with us next time.

The line at our counter is shorter.

We're all happy to herald that old Avis campaign as one of the greats. But how many of us are willing to admit to our market that we aren't the biggest brand?

We champion these old ads as feats of copywriting. And it's true, they're clever because they reframed a seemingly negative brand position as a positive.

But having tried to get companies to say interesting things for more than a decade, I now think the real triumph was getting the business to accept the reality of what it was.

Similarly, you may have seen some of the ads promoting a budget hostel in Amsterdam by the wonderful KesselsKramer. Instead of pretending their cheap accommodation was some sort of affordable luxury, they leaned into the fact that their facilities were of a lower quality.

These ads are an excellent example of spinning negative traits into a positive light by framing them in the right context.

But how many brands have the courage to embrace their shortcomings like this? How many marketers have the humility to have this much fun?

For a brief period of time McDonalds used to run ads about how healthy their menus were. I'm sure the legal department there ensured these were 'factual'. They were also bullshit.

Compare those to their more recent ads where people cheekily raise their eyebrows to signal they're grabbing their favourite guilty pleasure. That's truth. And it's a lot more memorable.

The pursuit of the truth is a valuable service

In many markets, the solutions people buy are just tools they need to uncover the truths that matter to them. In such cases, the best way to use your marketing resources is to devote them to the pursuit of those same truths. One of my favourite examples of this dynamic in B2B is from a company named Apptio.

In case you've never heard of them, Apptio make software that helps businesses understand what they're really spending on IT so they can figure out whether it's worth it or not.

In the early days of the business, it could be argued that the market for this software didn't even really exist. That's because most businesses had no idea how complex it was to figure out the reality of IT costs. They assumed it was like any other cost, a single entry in the year's books.

Nowadays, 'IT finance' teams are responsible for tracking, analysing and judging these costs. These are the folks who buy and use Apptio's software. But back then, no such teams actually existed. Some poor soul from finance or IT just rustled up a spreadsheet or ten and hoped they could make sense of the millions their companies spent on tech that year.

So when Apptio first took their novel software to market, they also set up an independent council for Technology Business Management. The role of this council was to bring together the people who were actually working on this non-trivial problem to collaboratively create standards that could be applied at any business.

This group of people effectively got together and invented the job that needed to be done.

In other words, they actively dedicated time and budget to the pursuit of the truth that mattered to the people they were selling to. It helped their buyers get specific about what they needed to solve this problem. It helped them make their own software better.

But the most magical thing to me is that it made a market where there was none. If the people that supposedly make up your market aren't actually talking to each other, it's not much of a market.

So when a company like Apptio demonstrates a public commitment to create a space where a group of like-minded people can seek the truth together, they're effectively nurturing a whole market into existence. The harder they commit to fostering a truth-seeking environment, the bigger their total addressable market grows.

It wasn't easy or obvious or even particularly convenient for them to run that council in a genuinely independent way. Yet ultimately, it's what stopped them from being just another startup with a cool-sounding bit of tech that not enough people paid for.

The truth is always welcome

It can be daunting trying to devise a communication strategy for a brand today. In so many ways, the scope of branded communications is a whole lot wider than it used be when Bernbach and Ogilvy were doing their thing.

But no matter what channel you're communicating in, what medium you're relying on or what budget you're working with, the truth is always a good place to start.

Because no matter how crowded, confusing and riddled with bullshit the modern marketing landscape seems to become, you can always be certain that it's a damn sight less crowded, confusing and full of bullshit than the information landscape our buyers find themselves in.

For the sake of the people who need to buy what you're selling, and for your own business' long-term position in the market, the truth is just better communication.

Part IV
So what do we do?

Truth-seeking as a marketing function

Some of the most valuable time I've spent in marketing has been the hours I've spent talking to my clients' customers. That's because no matter how much I think I know about the segment we're selling to or the solution we're selling them, customers are always just a little bit weirder than I think they'll be.

One of the most genuinely customer-curious companies I ever worked with makes project management software – the stuff you use to list out all the things that need to be done by a team so you can track the progress of multiple moving parts in one central location. It's pretty straightforward stuff.

Some years ago, their product management team was doing a round of customer interviews to understand how the people who really loved the software actually used it. You won't be surprised to learn that most of them used it to manage projects.

But one of their customers was a guy running a tiny service firm and he was using the software...as a CRM. He was using it as a database to track and manage all his client relationships too.

For the uninitiated, database products are designed to help you traverse long lists of people and details about them. Project management software, to put it bluntly, is designed so several people can update a big to-do list. This was a seriously weird way to use the product.

The upshot was that he absolutely loved it. While all the other customers they interviewed were happy to talk about how the software saved them money, this guy's experience was that it was making him money.

The truth is reliably weird

No one who worked at that company would have thought to use their product to manage customer relationships. Why would they?

Had they not been willing to talk to all those people, they'd never have found the one guy 'misusing' their product and they'd never have imagined the additional value they could be creating for everyone else. In fact, it inspired them to make a brand new CRM product that they now happily offer.

In my experience, every market is full of weird little surprises like this. And this kind of weirdness is exactly what we should be chasing after as marketers. It isn't always useful and by definition, it isn't common, apparent or easy to find. But the few times you do discover something this unusual, you also unlock unusual opportunities.

From the way some people talk about using AI and software in marketing, you'd think we operate in a perfectly logical domain where eventually there will no longer be any need for human beings.

As if all we'll need is some robot to sanction research from a bunch of other AI agents to trigger campaigns of auto-generated creative that can then be optimized through automated A/B tests which spit out dashboards and reports for, presumably, other robots to evaluate.

Maybe the tech will prove me wrong in the long run but for the world we live in now, I think that's a bunch of misguided nonsense.

Because the truth is that the markets we're selling to are ultimately just groups of people. And people do weird shit all the time. More important, it takes the curiosity of other people to make sense of all that weird shit.

No matter how fast or efficient or user-friendly our technology becomes, the essential weirdness inherent in how and why we buy things will always persist.

A personal and somewhat humiliating example: two weeks ago I visited the dental hygienist for the first time in about four years (I know, I'm disgusting, get over it). If you looked at my buying journey, it would appear to be fairly straightforward at first glance. I looked up dental hygienists near me on Google, found one that was a 30-minute walk from me, looked up some reviews and proceeded to register and pay them.

But what motivated me to spend money on this thing that I had avoided for literal years? My shoulders hurt.

I had probably just overdone it while climbing. But when I was in pain late at night, I got a little spooked about why exactly my shoulders hurt, remembered loosely a news story about a football player who overcame repeated injuries by getting a dental infection sorted, et voila, a dentist in Croydon made £79.

Now look, I'm not saying that dentists should start doing targeted campaigns for people with shoulder injuries. But I am saying that the only reason you know the truth about why I overcame such an intense mistrust of dentists (I remain convinced they're all serial killers) is because I was willing to tell you.

There is no substitute for talking to people.

The abiding value of having a chat

There is a certain efficiency to collecting vast amounts of quantitative research on how and why people buy. But people lie about what they believe and do all the time. Even in anonymized surveys, people routinely attempt to signal virtue, competence and bravado by buffing their answers up in some way or another.

So if you're trying to research something, it isn't enough to look for facts. We need to dig deeper and seek out truth. Even if it's squishy and abstract.

This is why conversations and qualitative research are so important. They give us an opportunity to hear what people will say about themselves while also revealing how people feel about the things they're willing to reveal.

You may not be able to create a neat little bar graph of how much pride someone feels in describing the way they solved a problem for themselves. And you won't find any dashboards capturing how scared someone feels when they try out a new way of working.

But seeing them feel that way may well shape everything about how and what you communicate to other people like them.

Three inter-related principles worth bearing in mind:

1. It matters when you interview them.
There's a big difference between interviewing someone at the start of your process and at the end of it. At the start of a process, a conversation with a customer is novel input. The things we hear will guide our thinking throughout the rest of the process. We're more open to our customers' sense of prioritization and more willing to be surprised by them.

Towards the end of a marketing process, these conversations turn more into validation sessions. We've already made our minds up about what matters having made a series of other decisions. So if the customer says something that's at odds with what the group of marketers now think, it's easy to dismiss it. Instead we ask leading questions hoping desperately that the answers will confirm everything else we think.

If you want to make sure you're discovering the truth as your customer sees it, it helps to go in when you don't have any baggage.

2. Conversations are better than interrogations.
Sometimes the salesperson or account owner responsible for the customer relationship is a little nervous about letting new people talk to them. They're worried it'll take some of the shine off the relationship. In cases like this, a common and seemingly reasonable ask is for a list of questions that'll be discussed.

The problem is that this can quickly turn into a robotic, monotonous grilling that leaves little room for surprise. It isn't how we talk to friends or dates or strangers at parties.

A good conversation is one where you're both genuinely interested in understanding each other. You want to keep it loose enough that your customer is free to brag and moan and confess to things they didn't expect to. And you want to give yourself the freedom to go wherever the conversation takes you.

If all the interviewer is doing is reciting a questionnaire, you should've just sent a questionnaire.

3. Everyone has a narrative.
This is particularly true when you're talking to media-trained executives but I think it's also true of ordinary consumers. We all have a story about ourselves or about how the world works that we'd really like to be true. These stories are designed to protect us from coming across as uncertain or fallible or stupid.

The problem is that like any story, these narratives become increasingly susceptible to bullshit the more they're told.

So the ideal environment for an honest conversation with a customer is therefore without an audience of colleagues and superiors. If you want to find surprising truths, people need to be able to contradict themselves and work out what they think without worrying if they sound good. The point of the conversation isn't to find good soundbites, it's to see how they really think, to discover what they actually do.

Marketing as an investigative unit

Modern marketing organizations pride themselves on how quickly they're adopting technology.

But if so much of the modern marketing leader's job is about organizing different teams and platforms and channels, how much room is left for them to actively investigate the reality of the markets they're serving? How much time could we be devoting to ethnography and other forms of customer research instead? How much should we?

I ask these as open questions because it would be foolish of me to be overly prescriptive about how you use your scarce resources. But they are at least worth pondering. So here's another one.

If you've heard of Clay Christensen's Jobs-to-be-done framework, you've likely heard of one of the canonical examples associated with it.

I'm referring to the story of how a fast food chain wanted to understand how it could sell more milkshakes, realized most milkshake purchases happened in the morning and found that most buyers felt a tall, thick shake was an ideal breakfast as they were driving to work.

It's a great story. But the reason we can talk about it is because someone spent several days sat down in a fast food restaurant with a notebook and pen, watched people come in to buy milkshakes and then chased after them to ask them why.

The question: are your marketing resources set up to do anything even remotely like that?

Do any of your people have the time or explicit mandate to sit and watch the people who buy from you?

Is anyone chasing after your customers to ask them why they're doing what they're doing?

Is this kind of investigation adequately prioritized?

Again, you might reasonably protest that this kind of thing is too expensive or out of the norm or even overwrought. And fair enough.

But if all we do is plumbing, plumbers we will be.

Truth is better marketing

Truth-telling as a marketing function

Chapter 9

The emergence of the internet changed marketing in a million different ways. But I believe the most important way it changed markets is still remarkably underrated.

Previously, when companies wanted to address the customers in their markets, they either needed to rent space in broadcast media or directly mail their target audience.

The internet, being a medium of many media, gave marketers the ability to do both those things, as well as a third thing: it gave birth to a new commons. A space that lives in the middle of all markets, independent of both buyers and sellers.

It's both the billboard and the town square all around it.

I believe that what's still underrated about this commons is that it is still a place people go to when they're looking for truth.

That might sound ludicrous given the internet's well-earned reputation as a source of misinformation. But I'd argue that precisely because the internet has exposed us to how much bullshit there is, it's also created an almighty appetite for truth.

I believe that's a pretty massive opportunity for marketers to attract the attention and interest of ideal prospects by publishing useful truths.

So long as we play by the rules of the commons.

The difference between advertising and publishing

Anything said in an ad will reasonably presumed to be bullshit. That is, anyone watching or reading or hearing an ad can tell from its tone and length that its contrived. These things are supposed to be hyperbolic and misleading and wrong in ways that are hard to spot.

They may not always be but when people come across them, their starting assumption is that there's going to be at least a little nonsense in there.

On the other hand, when something is published in a commons, people are generally doing it to connect with the other people gathered there. Even if it's a shitpost or a joke to troll the gullible, the intent is still communal.

So when you see a post online, you can generally assume someone wants you to know how they think. When you see an ad, you can generally assume you're seeing how a brand wants you to think.

I believe this is the salient difference between advertising through broadcast media and publishing in a commons. It's why an ad that contains some real human truth in it is inordinately more memorable. Meanwhile a post that cynically betrays the reader's trust is inordinately more repulsive.

To think like a broadcaster is to assume the audience is patiently waiting for you to shout something manipulative at them. It's this mindset that gets you a video of Kendall Jenner offering some troops a can of Pepsi during a culture war.

I assume it's also why you get so much cynical over-dichotomizing in online discourse from brands – marketing's naïve attempt at 'divide and conquer'. This is when you make up a false division amongst your audience and ask people to pick a side. Bullshit in its purest form.

I'm sure there are plenty of A/B tests that prove people click on buttons more often when you pull this kind of crap. But if this is the best we can come up with when exposed to a free, global con-

nection between people all over the planet, then we might as well pack it in as marketers.

The truth works

The flipside of this is that if a brand earnestly commits to sharing truth within a commons, it also stands to be inordinately rewarded.

Consumers and B2B buyers want to know the truths that are most relevant to them. Executives want to know how other executives are making decisions. They want to know if the impact of their strategies are real or not. Consumers want to know if the things they're buying will actually help them or not.

As brands become publishers, producing their own content and sharing it through their own channels, I think the real opportunity of the internet is to dedicate all those marketing resources to the spreading of truth.

The thing is, this isn't some hidden opportunity no one's tapped into. You can already plainly see the appetite for this kind of truth in marketing.

Spotify Wrapped shows how much it means to people to discover the truth about their own listening habits. My friends and I are so excited to share our top 5 artists because we're just as excited to find out who they really are.

Dove's Real Beauty campaign shows how much consumers of cosmetics appreciate a little honesty in a market otherwise dominated by glossy, superficial bullshit.

Chewy's much-lauded pet advice on Youtube shows how much a brand can gain from just earnestly explaining things that might be useful to their buyers.

Time and time again, earnest, truthful marketing cuts through the noise and helps businesses stand out. The gold standard of this approach is producing things that actually do something useful for an audience.

Stripe built a tool called Atlas that makes it easier for people to start online businesses in the US from anywhere in the world – furthering their mission of growing the GDP of the internet and guess what, earning them more customers.

Listerine sponsored the jet-washing of Mitchell Library in Glasgow earning a ton of positive impressions on social media and positively associating their brand with cleaning stuff up.

This is what it means to humbly make earnest contributions to the commons. To add value in a way that's aligned with the value your products are creating.

In all of these cases, the truth has proven to be a worthy guide for the marketing efforts of all these brands. And I'm sure you've encountered dozens more. So how might the truth guide you?

What quiet part can you say out loud?

What research could you do that your market would be grateful for?

What perspectives could you shine a light on to help your market think in new ways?

What concept could you explain that would help educate the people buying from you?

What tools can you build that might help your buyers accomplish their goals?

What problem can you solve that would create positive mental associations with your brand?

Show the market the market

This might sound banal compared to some of the more high-falutin' things we've talked about so far but when it comes to earnestly publishing the truth, I believe the lowest hanging fruit is to get good at telling your customers' stories. Yeah, case studies.

Case studies generally have a reputation as being bottom-of-the-funnel assets that you muster together in a hurry. In B2B, they usually follow a strict formula of 'Challenge-Solution-Results' and involve the rash cobbling together of whatever scraps of data you can get from customers, if you can get any at all.

But case studies are social proof. The thing a prospective customer cares most about is if people like them are making the same choice. How did it go for them? Are they glad they did it? Did doing this thing make them look like a fool?

When we shunt the only evidence that someone like our prospect bought from us into a contrived, 'snackable' format, we eliminate all traces of truth from it. It becomes immediately clear that whatever is left in the cookie-cutter summary is probably just a rosy version of the real story.

If nothing else, I believe marketers should be committing more of their budgets to artfully telling the whole story of their happiest customers. Film them, hang pictures of them from banners at your events, take soundbites from them and make them the centrepiece of your campaigns.

Show your market what it really looks like. Take the time to understand the people who buy from you and then invest as much time into showing everyone else how they think.

Showcase real people and real people just like them will tune in every time.

The catch

If telling the truth sounds like a straightforward strategy, let me reassure you that it's anything but. The thing that makes it tricky is that realistically, you'll only gain the benefits of doing all this is if you're committed to it in the long term.

Telling the truth once might get people to notice you. But telling a single lie can immediately dismantle your reputation too. Especially online.

Even trickier, we're all competing against a million other brands and people, all trying desperately to convince each other they're telling the truth. Some of them are full of shit and they may very well succeed in convincing your prospects that they're not.

Indeed, in the short term, you may very well lose out to some of the people who are instead willing to resort to dark UX patterns and manipulative messaging and bullshit broadcast thinking.

Realistically, for a prospect to realize your brand is actually committed to the truth, they'll probably need to have several interactions that reinforce that idea. There aren't really any shortcuts. It takes time to develop a reputation as an honest broker. It isn't enough to dip your toes in the water.

But the truth is a better way to promote yourself because in so many domains it remains largely uncontested. It is evidently far easier for most marketers to borrow the tone and style of something authentic than it is for them to actively do something real.

So precisely because of how inconvenient it is to commit to truth-telling as a long-term communication strategy, you stand to differentiate yourself from everyone else trying to growth hack their way to real human connection.

Like anything worth doing, it isn't easy. But when you need to differentiate, to stand out, to authentically connect, you won't go wrong if you consistently aim for the truth. And your market will thank you for it.

Truth is better marketing

Part V
If truth be told

The paradox of good service

One of the worst clients I've ever had sold a platform that automated administrative tasks for the world's biggest companies.

The founding team operated with a kind of arrogance, entitlement and uninformed impatience that I'd come to expect from well-funded companies in their sector so I couldn't really hold it against them.

But the thing that bummed me out about working with them was the glee with which they'd talk about how many people would be put out of a job by their platform.

Usually, people dance around the consequences of their automation. I've lost count of how many times I've written the words "...so your people can focus on more important things..." for SaaS products. Almost every single time what that really means is '...so you can fire 40% of your team.'

These guys, though, were giddy with pride. And they were pretty sure the executives who'd buy their platform would be downright ecstatic about it too, albeit in private.

The funny thing is, all these years later, I actually kind of admire their stance. Indeed, a small part of me wonders if, perhaps, the brand work we did would have been better if it had more accurately reflected the inherent sociopathy they operated with.

Maybe the executives we were selling to would have found it refreshing. Maybe I did them a disservice by writing copy that pussyfooted around what they actually meant. I can't know for sure.

But given I'm writing a book about the truth being better marketing, I feel like I should at least address the question of whether or not all truth is worth telling in a marketing context. So let me put it this way.

The very worst clients require the very best service

One of the more annoying things you realize after a decade in a service industry is that the clients you like the most, the ones you most enjoy working with, the ones who 'get it', are actually, in important ways, the people who need you the least.

They're so easy to work with because they already believe in doing things the way you do them. So logically, they'd probably do things that way whether you were involved or not.

On the other hand, the very worst clients, the ones who fight tooth and nail to operate in sub-optimal ways just because that's what they're used to, the ones who seem almost immune to expertise, they're the ones who actually need good advice the most.

This is the paradox of good service. It's a pain in my ass and if you offer any kind of service for a living, I'm sure it's a pain in yours too.

Because as much as I'd like to only give advice to people who agree with me all the time, the fact of the matter is that I stand to create the most value when I get through to the people who don't think the way I do.

So if you're operating in a company up to its neck in bullshit, or communicating in a space dominated by fluff and hyperbole, is it worth prioritizing the truth?

The more bullshit there is the more truth matters

If there is one question that has motivated me to write this book it's this: why, when the truth is so clearly better fodder for more effective marketing, is it such a novelty?

The simplest answer I can offer is that we default to bullshit because we're so thoroughly surrounded by it. Too often for too many of us in marketing, the safest path is to do the things that look and sound like the kind of marketing the rest of our category does.

As much as we talk about differentiation and standing out from the crowd, so much of how we work is designed to keep us looking like everyone else.

We collect references of each other's work, mimic each other's strategies and follow each other's 'best practices' as we rush from one bandwagon to the next, nervously avoiding big swings because we're so worried about big misses.

Years ago during a brainstorm at a well-known tech company I was working with, the senior-most marketing leader vetoed a wild idea someone suggested by saying, "we don't want to raise our heads too far above the parapet." I admire his honesty for saying what so many marketers would never admit.

But isn't it strange that marketers should feel the need to operate this way? If we aren't willing to take risks to get noticed, who will? Product? Legal? Compliance?

More importantly, if the safest thing you can do in your industry is to publish more bullshit cliches and empty fluff, I'd venture that isn't as safe a move as it seems. The things you won't get fired for doing don't neatly overlap with the things that'll help your business win.

We can codify and quantify and operationalize every proven tactic till we're blue in the face but at the end of the day, we cannot hide from the fact that to do great marketing we have to be willing to take some risks. I'd argue that pursuing the truth no matter where it takes us is precisely the kind of risk we should be willing to take.

Paradoxically, the riskier it feels to be led by the truth, the more worthwhile it is to follow it. The more the bullshit dominates our categories, the more we should be thinking about subverting it. The bigger the gap there is between what our markets think and what our industries are willing to admit, the more we should be willing to speak truth.

Not because it'll feel good, not so we may look righteous. Simply because the truth is a better guide for our strategies, a better beacon for our customers and a better way to reliably make more money for longer periods of time.

The truth about zagging

Some of the most expensive bullshit I've ever contributed to was, it likely won't surprise you, for a telco. Telcos are weird businesses because they deliver one of the most valuable things imaginable – connectivity – while still reeling from the fact that their oligopolies failed to imagine just how valuable it would be.

Everyone is simultaneously making more money than they should be and also somehow less money than they could be.

This triggers a series of strange competitive dynamics for the industry. The strangest of which is how frantically every telco ove-rhypes every new generation of connectivity in the vague hope that they may finally get to charge a premium for the service they deliver. My misfortune was to help one of these businesses scream very loudly about the launch of 5G.

It was going to revolutionize everything about the way everything works! By golly, every industry would be completely flip-turned upside down by just how quickly they could move data around! You wouldn't believe how much more was possible!

In the end, like every other launch of every other generation of connectivity, most of the hype was bullshit. The use cases we were excitedly telling the world about didn't actually materialize into anything particularly noteworthy. And most of the technologies we were bragging about transforming ended up doing just as well without any help from the telcos.

The actual value created by 5G is still utterly dwarfed by the noise made about it.

The funny thing is, we knew it would be. The whole time we were working day and night on that campaign, all the smart, talented marketers I worked with knew that we were overegging that cake. We knew how over the top our claims were. We knew it wasn't going to resonate with the wider world because why on earth would it?

And yet we did it anyway. Why? Because all the other telcos were doing it. Because that's what telcos do. Because if we didn't do it, the other guys might benefit from doing it. And we weren't going to let that happen.

I'd venture that any telco with the wherewithal to resist that frenzy would have done at least as well during that time for a fraction of the cost. The relative value of the excess share of voice would be higher once everyone else's campaigns had slowed back down and you'd probably have sold just as much 5G (barely any).

At a time when everyone was trying desperately to make fetch happen, the glaring opportunity for any telco was to position themselves as the only ones being calm and realistic about the new technology. Did anyone take it? Not a one.

Because the thing no one tells you about zagging when everyone else is zigging is how much it feels like losing. It's easy for me to say you don't need to participate in a pointless race to spend as much money as everyone else. It's much harder to muster the courage, vision and commitment to do it.

The paradox of good marketing is that the lonesome fear you feel when you're zagging is actually a sign that you're on the right path.

Two truths about marketing

Chapter 11

When I was younger, I believed that idealism inevitably fades. That my belief in values like honour, integrity and honesty would look increasingly childish the more I brushed up against the reality of the world.

But the older I've gotten, the more I've come to appreciate what a load of nonsense that is.

For starters, there's nothing romantic about committing to the truth. It's just a practical way to make sure you're on a path to creating real value. As much of a pain in the ass as it is, the truth solves our biggest problems.

• It helps you build strategies that can actually win because they're based on the very real imperfections that shape your business.
• It guides you to more accurately identify who you're right for so you can speak to them more clearly.
• It allows the people you work with to more plainly address the problems they're facing so they can actually do something about them.

Honour, integrity and honesty aren't just fluffy ideals. They're values that bind us to the people we're selling to so we may continue to sell to them in the long run.

Previously in this little book I said that no one gets into marketing because they're pursuing the truth. The thing is, I don't believe most of us got into marketing because we were explicitly pursuing bullshit either.

I think we settled for it.

I think that over time a million little compromises chipped away at our internal compasses till all that was left was a metastasized vocabulary of bullshit. So we ended up clinging to whatever half-truths and lies would help us get ahead by toeing imaginary company lines.

The result is that even though no one is explicitly flying the flag for bullshit being the right approach to marketing, we're in an industry overflowing with it.

Between the replication crisis in behavioural science, the unanswered claims of widespread ad fraud in online media and all the tone-deaf chest-thumping on linkedin, it's becoming harder and harder to deny that bullshit isn't the primary currency in marketing.

For truth to prevail, we need to first learn to tolerate two unimpeachable, yet somehow largely unspoken, truths about what we do.

Truth #1: There is no such thing as a sure thing.
No tactic, no model, no framework, no hack can guarantee success in marketing.

That certainty we so frequently default to when we're trying to persuade our clients and CEOs to do things is nothing more than an illusory attempt to make the future feel comfortable. But it isn't. The future is and always will be uncertain, unpredictable, surprising.

To pretend otherwise is to ignore the fundamental nature of reality itself.

Even with all my conviction in the value of honest marketing, I have to admit that there will be some situations where bullshit will sell more product. Where something I recommended you do in this book just doesn't work. That's just how this goes.

The truth is that none of us is above the whims of the wider world we're just one small part of. Our markets will do what they think is right for them, whether we like it or not. To tolerate this unpredictability, we have to be open to whatever weird outcomes we discover. Prepared to adapt to whatever we learn. Friendly to the inherent uncertainty of everything we do.

The truth is better marketing because at the end of the day, if we're perfectly honest with ourselves, none of us know if any of this shit will actually work or not.

That's not an indictment of what we're doing, it's just how the world really works. Rather than fearing this and retreating to a false certainty we should feel humbled by it, liberated to take more risks and try more novel things. If we only try things in some vain attempt to prove we were right along, the only certainty is that we'll make fools of ourselves.

The truth is weird and hard to get to, but it's ultimately the only way we can know that what we're cooking up in our decks has some relation to what happens in the minds of the people we're selling to. The more humility we show in the face of it, the more fun it is to find out what it is.

Truth #2: If you don't prioritize the truth, no one else will.
So here's something true I'm not that thrilled to admit: if you hired me to write some bullshit for you, there's a good chance I'd do it. (Visit www.harendrakapurb2b.com!)

As much as I believe the truth is better marketing, and as much as I'll always try my best to guide my clients in the direction I believe will be most effective, at the end of the day I'm hired to do what you believe is the right thing to do. I won't write the truth if you explicitly pay me not to.

And when push comes to shove, if you make me choose between being a broke pain in your ass and paying my bills, I'd be an idiot for not choosing the latter.

There is certainly integrity in refusing work on principle. I've done it before and I'll gladly do it again. But, in my book, there's also a lack of integrity in wasting someone's time and money just because they aren't doing everything exactly the way I want them to.

So if that involves spinning some half-truths into credible-sounding bullshit when we're several weeks deep into a process with a tight deadline around the corner, yeah, I'll probably do it, take your money and hope we don't cross paths again.

My point isn't to flaunt what a massive hypocrite I'm willing to be when I need to. It's that if the marketers driving the process aren't committed to going where the truth takes them, you can't reasonably expect the people you hire to fight for it indefinitely.

If you brief your agency on some faffy nonsense about your goals and target audience, you'll probably get some bullshit back from them. Sure, it'd be nice if you could trust everyone you hire to keep you honest. But people like me will only ever keep you as honest as we think you really want to be.

There are a million invisible opportunities to compromise on the truth throughout any marketing process. So if you want to make the truth a priority, you have to take responsibility for it, no matter how messy, confusing or inconvenient it turns out to be.

That means accounting for how fallible our appetite for the truth really is. At any given point in a process it's worth asking:

- Are we seeking truth or consensus?
- Are we using data for validation or illumination?
- Are we seeing things as they are or as we wish they were?
- Are we telling the truth or just blowing sunshine up our market's butt?
- Are we really telling the 'truth in advance' or bluffing our way forward?

Following the truth wherever it takes you requires a sequence of skills. Sifting through the data you've collected for truth is a skill. Addressing the truth in a tricky conversation is a skill. Reiterating the truth so a whole team adhere to it is a skill. Running towards problems is a skill. Defining a strategy based on hard choices is a skill.

Each one of these skills can take a lifetime of practice to master. But ultimately these are the skills that we need to deliver a good service. To do good marketing.

A moment for truth

I think the truth has always been a better approach to marketing. But I really believe we live in a time where businesses stand to be rewarded more richly than ever before for committing to the truth.

The markets we're selling to are more bamboozled by bullshit than they've ever been. And the mechanisms for rewarding earnest brands are more robust than they've ever been.

Yet, while I do believe the world would be a better place if the marketing community stopped the global arms race to produce more bullshit, I don't expect that to happen any time soon. Certainly not because I wrote some words down.

But the more businesses start to build their brands on the basis of something real, the harder it will be for bullshit to win. So if telling the truth about your products won't help you sell more of them, I'd say you have far bigger problems than communication. And it might be time to start fixing them.

My hope with writing this book is that you already felt this way about the truth. That the stories I've shared here and the points I've made have helped reinforce your own belief in following the truth wherever it may take you. As I've said previously, my goal isn't to convince you of anything, it's to reassure you that you aren't the only one thinking this way.

Ordinarily, I'd be trying to wrap this up with some sort of rousing call to arms. But the truth is, I don't really believe we need some sort of revolution to champion the truth. In fact, for those of us who do believe in it, it'd arguably be easier to stand out if the bullshit artists keep doing their thing.

I just think that if more marketers humbly followed the truth and devoted more resources to earnestly conveying it to their markets, they'd make more money, keep their jobs a while longer and probably have a little more fun doing them.

Ultimately, the prize for following the truth isn't to restore marketing to some former glory that probably never even existed. It isn't to pat ourselves on the back.

It is to simply create more value, for longer periods of time.

*

Printed in Great Britain
by Amazon

52563954R00056